The Romani Collection

Dukh — Pain

SERIES EDITOR: AGGOTT HÖNSCH ISTVÁN

THE ROMANI COLLECTION

DUKH — PAIN

HEDINA TAHIROVIĆ SIJERČIĆ

MAGORIA BOOKS

2007

Published by MAGORIA BOOKS

© Copyright 2007 Hedina Tahirović Sijerčić

All rights reserved. No part of this book may be used or reproduced in any manner without the written permission of the Publisher.

Dukh — Pain by Hedina Tahirović Sijerčić

First Edition

ISBN 978-0-9781707-5-2

www.MagoriaBooks.com

HEDINA TAHIROVIĆ SIJERČIĆ was born on 11. 11. 1960. in Sarajevo, Bosnia and Herzegovina. She is a graduate journalist and teacher. She organized and hosted Romani programs for the Radio-TV station in Sarajevo and worked as an activist for The International Romani Union. She later lived in Toronto and worked as a teacher for the Toronto District School Board. While in Canada she was the Editor-in-Chief of the first Canadian-Romani newsletter, *Romano Lil* from 1998 to 2001.

She was a Canadian delegate at the World Conference against Racism, Racial Discrimination and Xenophobia: Forum of the Americans in 2001 at Quito, Ecuador. At the moment she is living in Germany.

Hedina is the author of the book *Romany Legends* with the texts in English and German, 2004, Turnshare, London, England and she translated the book *How we live* from Bosnian to Romani, 2001, Bosnia and Herzegovina. She was also the editor-in-chief of, and one of the contributing authors in, the booklet *Kanadake Romane Mirikle (Canadian Romani Pearls)* 1999, Toronto. She also translated the book *Ilmihal* from Serbo-Croatian to Romani, 1995, Sarajevo. In 1991, Hedina translated a feature film *Ratvali bijav (Boda de Sangre)* by Garcia Lorca from Romani to Serbo-Croatian. She was also a writer/editor of two documentary films: *Adjive Romen* and *Karankoci-Koci*, TV Sarajevo, 1989.

* * *

HEDINA TAHIROVIĆ SIJERČIĆ bijandili 11. 11. 1960. ando Saraj (Sarajevo), Bosna thaj Hercegovina. Voj si sikadi zhurnalisti thaj uchitelka-sikamni. Hedina sasa angluni editori pala Romane programe pe Radio-Televizijate Sarajevo, thaj aktivisti ande Internacionalna Romani Organizacija. Voj dzuvdili ande Torontoneste kaj resli Ontario Koledj- Vuchi Sikamni Diploma. Voj cherdja buchi ande Toronto sar regularni sikamni pe Engliski chib pala skolaki themeski organizacija pe anav Toronto District School Board. Hedina sasa angluni editori pala angluno Romano lil ande Kanada pe akhardipe *Romano Lil*, 1998-2001.

Voj sasa Kanadaki delegati pe Themeski Konferencija pala antirasizam thaj diskriminacija, 2001, ande Quito, Ekvador, (Juzhna Amerika). Hedina akana dzuvdel ande Germanija.

Hedina romasarda *Romany Legends* ande Engliski chib, 2004, Engleska, London. Gova lil ikljovel dujchibeski, ande Engleski-Germanski chib. Hedina tradili o lil *Gova si amaro dzuvdipe, na dzanen aver* katari Bosanski chib ande Romani chib, 2001, Bosna thaj Hercegovina. Voj si editori thaj autori pala o lil *Kanadake Romane Mirikle*, 1999, Toronto, Kanada. Hedina tradili o lil *Ilmihal* katari Serbsko-Hrvacki chib ande Romani chib, 1995, Saraj, TV filmo *Ratvali bijav* kataro G.Lorka katari Romani ande Serbsko-Hrvacki chib, 1991. Hedina si autori thaj editori pala duj dokumentarno TV-filmo *Adjive Romen* thaj *Karankochi-Kochi*, TV Sarajevo, 1989.

English and Romani Lector: Ronald Lee
Cover Illustrations: Rizah Sijerčić

Contents · Istardipe

"Good Afternoon, Roma!"	2
Lacho Djive Romalen	3
I Flee	4
Nashav	5
Life	6
Dzuvdipe	7
Sorrow	8
Dukhalipe	9
Calling Father's Soul	10
Akharipe e Dadeske Odji	11
Amanet for Daughter	14
Amanet Chejache	16
Mother	18
Daje	19
At Night	20
Rachako	21
Painful Magic	22
Dukhadi Madjija	23
Fortune-Teller	24
Drabarni	25
Romani Milky Way	26
Romano Thudalo Dromoro	27
Dream I.	28
Suno I.	30
Dream II.	34
Suno II.	38
Wind	42
Balval	43
Why?	44
Sose?	45
The Earth	46
Phuv	47
I Will Die For You	48
Ka Merav Pala Tute	49
I Have To Go From Here	50
Mora Te Dzav-Tar Katar	51
A Deceased Good Rom	54
Mulo Lacho Rom	55

Foreword

By Ronald Lee
Sessional Instructor
The Romani Diaspora
NEW343H1S
New College
University of Toronto

As an author, educator, journalist and poet, I find Hedina's poetry both impressive and evocative. She speaks of the beauty of Romani life in her former *Mahala* or Romani Quarter in Sarajevo, named a Sister City of my own Montreal in happier times, and a once beautiful centre of culture which was mindlessly destroyed during the ethnic and religious strife in Bosnia. She gives us an insight into this tragedy and her own pain and suffering at this loss. Since her arrival in Canada, she had worked tirelessly both to improve her own situation and to help her fellow Roma. She was editor in chief of our first Romani publication in Canada, *Romano Lil*, and worked as a parent-teacher liaison worker under a grant funded by Heritage Canada to help integrate the children of Romani refugees in Canada into the Canadian school system in Toronto. She also worked as a volunteer helping to organize Romani events in Toronto. In 1999, she edited the first booklet of Romani poetry in Canada, *Kanadake Romane Mirikle (Canadian Romani Pearls)*, an anthology which contained some of her own poems along with those of other Canadian Roma. This new collection of poems by Hedina, is also a milestone, the first time a Romani poet has ever written a collection of poems in *Gurbeti* Romani with English translations.

As a Canadian Rom, I fully recommend her work as an example of Romani poetry which speaks of the tragedy facing the Roma in the persecuting countries of central-eastern Europe and of her own feelings as a Romani woman who has experienced this traumatic but unknown episode of Romani history firsthand. Her poems describing Romani life and Romani folk beliefs are also valuable and will help non-Roma to understand the culture and customs of the Roma. She has created a valuable piece of our cultural heritage and I commend her for her dedication and talent.

Swaturya Mai Anglune Kaldershitskones

Katar o Ronald Lee
Instruktori Semestralno
E Romani Diaspora Ande Kanada
NEW343H1S
Universitato Torontosko
Toronto

Shavale, Rromale! Me sim Rrom Kanadako thai arakhadyilem ando kako them. Amé, le Rroma ande Kanada, chi mai xalyam o nekazo thai e persekutsiya kai xale amare Rromane phrala thai phenya ande Ivropa kai le Rroma musai te trayin ande phari miseriya thai diskriminatsiya. Ande'l neve dimokrasiyi ande Ivropa chintralno thai lasariyesko, le Gazhe akushen, maren, thai mudaren le Rromen. Phabaren lenge khera thai le kokalune shere (skini) thai e nevi kali leyiga (fashisturya) vorritsin le Rromen thai mudaren len po than. But Rromane azilanturya aven akana ande Kanada katar kakale thema. Me arakhlem but lendar thai ashundem penge historiyande. Murri amalní, E Hedina, si yekh lendar, Rromni sikadí thai godjaver, kai xalyas but nekazo le Gazhendar ando lako them. Musai sas lake te nashel lake themestar te rodel azilo politikalno ande Kanada te beshel ando liberto laka familiyasa.

Ande lake gilyá, E Hedina del-duma katar o yilo. Phenel amenge so dikhlas mashkar le Rroma ando Sarai thai ande Bosniya, ande peski Mahala ka prepedisardé le Gazhe ando lengo Gazhikano marimos kana mudardyile but Rroma. Le Rroma anda o Sarai thai anda e Bosniya. Musai-sas lenge te nashen-pe ka 'l avre thema Ivropanoske kai konik chi manglas te den le andré. But nashlé-pe ande Nyamptsiya thai ande Italiya. E Hedina sas baxtalí. Woi arakhlas azilantomos ande Kanada. Ando kako them, woi kerdyas buki te azhutil-pe thai te azhutil avre Rromene azulanturyen. Woi sas redaktórka-sherutni vash amari mai angluni Rromani publikatsiya ande Kanada, *Romano Lil*. Woi kerdyas o liloró, *Kanadake Romane Mirikle*, yekh kidemos amare Rromane gilyandar. Woi kerdyas buki ando amaro programo te azhutis le Romane shavoren ande wushkala ando Toronto. Kerdyas bari buki sar aktivista te pomozhil le Romen, desar woi avilyas ande Kanada.

Kako nevo lil katar E Hedina si o pervo data ande lumya ke ramosardyas yekh poeta Romani ekh kidemos peske gilyandar Romanes thai Inglezitskanes. Woi vorbil ando chisto glaso Rromano. Woi kerdyas bari buki. Te del o Del ke kako lil azhutil le Rromen, te zhanen mai mishto le Gazhe kon si le Rroma thai so si amari kultura, amaro trayo thai amari historiya.

Akana, woi geli pálpale ande Nyamptsiya kai beshel laka familiyasa. Te del o Del lake baxt, sastimus thai lungo trayo.

Introduction

These poems will be greatly appreciated by anyone with even a little interest or sensitivity to other cultures. The Romani culture carries a lot of mystery to the Gadze (non-Roma), and the authenticity and tenderness with which Hedina writes depicts the Romani world to us in an enlightening and endearing way. The specific personal experiences saturated by the effects of the Bosnian war shatter our illusions of a happy fantasy folk unperturbed and impenetrable by the effects of the foolish and cruel outside human and political world. As our lives have continued to collide historically and geographically, we find ourselves finally united personally through a rich human pathos expressed in poetry.

I earnestly hope we will be offered more of such writing, that we may see our common human soul though reflected in a traditional universe unfamiliar to us.

H. Laurel Peters
Canadian educator and
Balkan humanitarian aid worker

dukh pain

"Good Afternoon, Roma!"

In a dream
I am producing a radio-program in Romani.
I am listening to my voice:
"Good afternoon, Roma and children!
Good health and luck to you!"
Studio, microphone, music.
Gadze[1] dance with us.
Gadze laugh with us.
I am happy.

In a dream
I am producing a radio-program in Romani.
I am listening to my voice:
"Flee Roma! Flee children!
Flee as far as you can!"
Bombs, guns, knives.
The Gadze beat us.
The Gadze kill us.
I am devastated.

---

[1] *Gadze:* non-Roma people

Lacho Djive Romalen

Ando suno
Cherav radio emisija pe Romani chib.
Ashunav pesko krlo:
"Lacho djive, Romalen thaj chavalen!
Aven saste thaj bahtale!"
Studio, mikrofono, bashalipe.
E gadze chelen amenca.
E gadze hasaven amenca.
Bahtali sem.

Ando suno
Cherav radio emisija pe Romani chib.
Ashunav pesko krlo:
"Nashen dural Romalen thaj chavalen!
Nashen dur dural!"
Granaturja, jagala, churika.
E gadze maren amen.
E gadze mudaren amen.
Bibaxtali sem.

I Flee

I flee over the meadows and mountains
Driven away by a terrible noise.
I flee over the brooks and rivers
Driven on by the terrible noise.
Big-headed, winged, red insects bite me.
Black worms suck me.
Slimy moss imprisons me.
Red flowers stick to me.
I am falling down. I am running away.
I am falling down. I am running away.
Black, thick, dirty water swallows me.
I am choking.
The winged Romany bird rescues me,
And takes me into the white world.

Nashav

Nashav prdal pe livadjina thaj plajinaka
Von chingaren thaj traden man.
Nashav prdal pe pajorra thaj dorjava
Von chingaren thaj traden man.
Shorale, phakale, lole guguja dandalen man.
Kale cherma crden man.
Limali, lenaki char phangel man.
Loli, lenaki luludji pusavel man.
Perav. Nashav.
Perav. Nashav.
Melalo, kalo, chichidino pajorro nakhavel man.
Tasavav ma.
Romani, phakali chirikli ikalel man,
Ando parno them idjarel man.

Life

Life expires.
Life and luck,
Life and sorrow,
Life and time.

Man lives.
Man and home,
Man and children,
Man and poverty.

Wandering continues.
Wandering - other countries,
Wandering - other peoples,
Wandering - same damnation.

Loneliness remains.
Loneliness and sadness,
Loneliness and illness,
Loneliness and death.

Dzuvdipe

Dzuvdipe nakhel.
Dzuvdipe thaj bax,
Dzuvdipe thaj dukh,
Dzuvdipe thaj vakto.

Manush dzuvdel.
Manush thaj cher,
Manush thaj chavre,
Manush thaj chororipe.

Phiravipe lundjarel.
Phiravipe - aver phuvja,
Phiravipe - aver manusha,
Phiravipe - jekh armaja.

Korkoripe achel.
Korkoripe thaj dukhalipe,
Korkoripe thaj nasvalipe,
Korkoripe thaj mulipe.

Sorrow

Sorrow has enwrapped my soul,
my soul is suffocating.
As I breathe a poisoned air,
as I drink poisoned water,
I am suffocating.
My soul is suffocating.
Sorrow has enwrapped it.
As someone else lives
instead of me.
As someone else talks
instead of me.
As someone else walks
instead of me.

I am a stranger to myself.
And my heart, bloody, cries.
My tears are going to melt it.
The question I ask is:
when will it melt completely?
I have become a machine which breathes
And I ask myself:
Can sorrow enshroud a robot?

Sorrow has engulfed my soul,
it is suffocating.
Sorrow has smothered my soul,
and it is sinking.

Dukhalipe

O dukhalipe vulisarilo mrni odji,
odji tasavel pes.
Sar te phurdav drabardi hava,
sar te pijav drabardo paj,
me tasajvav.
Mrni odji tasavel pes.
O dukhalipe vulisarilo las.
Sar te vareko aver
andothan man dzuvdel.
Sar te vareko aver
andothan man vacharel.
Sar te vareko aver
andothan man phirel.

Themni sem korkori peske.
Mo ilo ratvalo rovel.
Jasva chinen les.
Phuchipe si kana ka pirosaren sasto.
Cherdivav mashina savi phurdel
Thaj me phuchav pes:
Shaj o dukhalipe te vulisarel trujal e robotesko?

O dukhalipe vulisarilo mrni odji,
odji tasavel pes.
O dukhalipe vulisarilo mrni odji,
odji tasavili.

Calling Father's Soul

Father help me!
Our souls — one soul.
Only you have forced me
to unwrap the sorrow which has engulfed me.
Only you have forced me
to stop the bloody tears of my heart.
Only you have forced me
to drive away a nightmare.
Father help me!
Our souls - one soul.
Only your soul can call my soul.
Call it father! I am suffocating!
Your life alone can call my life.
Call it father! I am dying!

Akharipe e Dadeske Odji

Dade dema va!
Amare odja - jekh odji.
Numaj tu ichares zuralipe te
putares pharipe savo vulisarilo man.
Numaj tu ichares zuralipe te
achaves ratvale jasva e morestar ilestar.
Numaj tu ichares zuralipe te
nashales moraki rakli.
Dade dema va!
Amare odja - jekh odji.
Numaj chiri odji shaj te akharel mrni.
Akhar dade, ka tasav!
Numaj chiro dzuvdipe shaj te akharel mrno.
Akhar dade, ka merav!

dukh

pain

Amanet[2] for Daughter

After child-birth, daughter of mine,
For forty days
Because of the charm,
Do not leave the house at twilight.
For forty days
Do not take your child outdoors,
Apply soot to his forehead.
For forty days
Fasten around your wrist and the child's
a crimson ribbon.

For forty days
Hide your child from the evil eyes,
And permit him not in the presence
Of an unclean woman.
Daughter of mine,
Guard your child and yourself
from the evil eyes
Or you may fall sick without hope of a cure.
And never,
Never pour out the bathwater at twilight
In an unclean place,
Or the water in which you washed
The diapers of your child.
Never ever,
Leave the diapers outside at night.
Never ever,
Extinguish the lamp during the night
Or ever permit your child
To cry very much.

---

[2] *amanet*: a charge entrusted to, endowed upon someone

And to you, daughter of mine,
I endow this charge
If someone hexes your child
Wipe him three times with your skirt
Spit three times upon his legs and say:
"I am your mother, I cannot curse you.
Evil eyes saw you and cursed you.
May the hex return to the one who cast it!
Sickness! Trouble!
Flee from my child!
Begone!
And go to the one who sent you!
Go to the Evil Eyes!"

Listen, daughter of mine,
To whom I endow this charge
Be a true Romani mother,
And watch over your children
Like an protective amulet.
Nurse them, caress them,
And with your own milk, heal them.

Be a true Romani mother,
And to the end of your life
Teach them of our ways,
The ways of our people,
Teach them their mother tongue.
Mark well every word
Never forget it
And tell them to your daughter
As I told you.
Endow her with the charge
As I endow you.

Amanet Chejache

Kana bijandes chavo, miri chaje,
pala jakhalipe,
starvardesh djivengo
na dza avri pe akshamo.
Starvardesh djivengo
na dza avri.
Thov funedjija pe chavoresko chikateste.
Shtarvardesh djivengo
thov pese thaj e chavorese loli fasha
trujal e vastengo.

Shtarvardesh djivengo
garudi chavo e dzungalende jakhende,
thaj na del e melale dzuvljendje te dikhel les.
Chaje,
arakh chavo thaj pes e plavo-zeleno jakhendar
shaj te nasvalen thaj nikana sastiven.
Nikana
na rispi ando akshamo, pe melale thanendje
pajoro ando savo san thodine chavoreske skuteke.
Nikana,
na muk skutore avri prdal pe racha.
Nikana
na mudar meljachi jagorri prdal pe rachako,
thaj na muk chavo but te rovel.

A tu, chaje,
me mukav tuche ando amanet:
Ako si chavo jakhaldo
thaj but rovel
khos les trin droma e piresa chohasa,
trin droma chung pe chavoreske prne thaj phend:
"Tuche dej sem, nashti te jakhalav tut.
Dzungalenge jakha jakhalel tut.
Jakhalipe, dza palpale ande Dzungalenge jakha.
Nash Nasvalo! Nash Melalo!
Nash e chavorestar! Nash! Dza ande dzungalenge jakha!"

Ashun, chejori,
mukav tuche ando amanet:
Av lachi Romani dej,
arakh pire chavoren
sar amajlija.
Chuchi del lendje, lachimasa del lendje.
E piresa thuvdensa sastiven len.

Av lachi Romani dej
dziko mulipeste.
Phend chavorenge kataro amanet, kataro amaro narodo.
Vachar lenca Romanes.
Ichar gova pe godji
Thaj thoska phend pire chejache,
muk lache ando amanet
sar me tuche.

Mother

In a dream my child speaks,
awake, he doesn't want to speak.
Mother, mother what should I do?
My child cries,
I do not know what his pain is.

His breast is swollen,
his eyes — bloodshot.
Mother, mother, what should I do?
My child cries,
his forehead burns.

Daughter! Daughter!
Mora[3] pulls at him.
She tears his dream,
She drinks his power.
Drive away the choxana!

---

[3]*mora*: a night butterfly, also called a *choxana*. The choxana comes to suck the blood of children which causes them to cry and become ill. She always comes at night because she is afraid of the daylight.

Daje

Ando suno mo chavo phenela,
vazdinjalo na mangela.
Daje, daje so te cherav me?
Mo chavo rovela,
na dzanava so les dukhela.

Leske chucha shuvljarde,
leske jakha ratvarde.
Daje, daje so te cherav me?
Mo ciknorro rovela,
lesko chikat tatarela.

Chaje, chaje,
Mora crdela les.
Voj phagela lesko suno,
Voj pijela lesko zor.
Xut e choxana!

At Night

I am going to leave the lamp on
next to the cradle.
I am going to rub a garlic clove
over the child's breast.

I am going to put the broom
behind the door.
I am going to pray to God.

To drive away the child's crying,
To drive away the bloodsucking butterfly,
The vampire moth - a *choxana*.

Rachako

Ka thovav e jagali memelin
pasha e kunate.
Ka thovav e parni purum
pe chavoreske chuchorate.

Ka thovav e shulavdi
pala udaresko
Ka rudjavav e rudjipe Devlesko.

Te nashalav e chavoresko rovipe,
Te nashalav las,
E choxana.

Painful Magic

Evils eyes are looking at you
Like rampaging water
They will destroy you.
Illness! - Begone
From your head
From your chest
From your hands
From your stomach
From your legs
Begone!
Back into the evil eyes!

Two eyes
Two hands
Two legs
Pain in the eyes
Go away into the legs
Go away from the legs
Into the earth.

Go away from the earth
Into death.
Go away!

Dukhadi Madjija

E dzungalenge jakha dikhen tut
Sar o paj mudaren tut!
Nasvalipe-nash tutar!
Andare chire shorestar
Andare chire kolinestar
Andare chire vastendar
Andare chire porestar
Andare chire prnalendar
Nash tutar,
Ando dzungale jakha!

Duj jakha
Duj vasta
Duj prnala
E jakhesko dukh
Dza ando prnalende
Dza andare prnalendar
Ande phuvjate.

Dza andare phuvjatar
Ando mulipeste!
Nash!

Fortune-Teller

From inside this cup
I will tell of your luck.

Don't look at me so sad
Things aren't so bad.

I have some magic
I see something tragic.

There is a guy
He makes you cry.

Don't look so sad
It isn't so bad.

Under the cup, just put some money
And it will work to bring a new honey.

You will fall in love
He will be your slave.

Under the cup, put your golden ring
And you will marry him in the spring.

I see a pram, a cradle, a toy
A crow, another woman, and a boy.

I have some magic
I see something tragic.

Don't look so sad
It isn't so bad.

Put your necklace under the cup
And a Romani bird will protect your luck.

Press your finger on the bitch
And things will go without a hitch
All will work out as you wish.

I see a foot, a dog, a boy
Now you'll be reunited in joy.

Drabarni

Ando fildzano me dikhav
Tuche e bax te vacharav.

Na dikh man dukhalo
Naj si sa dzungalo.

Hi man e choxanipe
Me dikhav e dukhalipe.

Kate si o mursh
Vov anel e dukhado brsh.

Na dikh man dukhalo
Naj si sa dzungalo.

Thov talo fildzano cira love
Ka cherel pala nevo patave.

Ka peres andi kamlimata
Von ka avel sar andi phandimata.

Thov talo fildzano sumnakuni angrusti
Ka cherel tut abijavehchi luludji.

Dikhav e vordon, e kuna, e chavoro
Kali khanji, aver Romni thaj murshoro.

Hi man e choxanipe
Me dikhav e dukhalipe.

Na dikh man dukhalo
Naj si sa dzungalo.

Thov talo fildzano sumnakuni merikli
Ka arakhel tut Romani chirikli.

Phajrar o naj prdal pe kurva
Chichind e jakha
E gindese del phaka.

Dikhav e dzukel, e prno, e chavorro
Gova dzangljol-pe jekhethane, gugloro.

Romani Milky Way

God desired and urged
That the Earth and Water marry.
The Earth and Water sought from God
A male child, a Sun, from their hearts.
The Earth conceived five times
And bore five daughters, five stars:
The first star — Flower
The second star — Faith
The third star — Apple
The fourth Star — Bird
The fifth Star — Hope
The Earth and Water cried
For they wanted a male child, the Sun.
God listened to them and said:
"Then make a solemn vow!
That every year you will slaughter a sheep,
Put its crimson blood on the child's forehead
And give him the name, Bread!"
The Earth and Water wept with joy and declared:
"It is our solemn vow!"

Romano Thudalo Dromoro

O Devel mangel thaj cherel
Kaj I Phuv thaj o Paj ansuren.
I Phuv thaj o Paj roden e Devlestar
Jekh murshikano chavo, o Kham, ilestar.
I Phuv khamnisajlel pandz dromengo
Thaj bijandili pandz chejango, chehrajango:
Prvi chehrajin – Luludji
Dujti chehrajin – Pachape
Triti chehrajin – Phabaj
Shtarti chehrajin – Chirikli
Pandzti chehrajin – Dozacharipe
I Phuv e Pajensa roven
Jekh murshikano chavo, o Kham, mangen.
O Devel ashunel thaj phendel:
"Dema sovli!
Neka sako brsh perel e bakresko shoro,
Thoven pe chavoresko chikateste e bakresko rat lolo.
Thaj akharen les Mahno."
I Phuv e Pajensa e baxtalipestar roven thaj phenden:
"Amen xan sovli!"

Dream I.

I am in my Romani Quarter
In Gorica, on Dajanli Osmanbega Street.
I am happy.
Ragged children around me,
The happy, tattered, neighbourhood Romani children
All around me.
I am happy.
I have many glittering candies
Dirty little hands reach for them
Warm black eyes yearn for them
Pretty red mouths devour them
All the Roma are in the Quarter
No one works
As usual.
The surroundings are beautiful.
Women's bright Turkish pantaloons sweep by
As do men's old, colourful shirts
Barefoot children running barely-clad,
with warm Romani hearts,
among the garbage,
amid the poverty.
Dirty, dusty, poor, bright, and happy.
Many Roma sit on the ground,
Conversing, laughing
Inside, each listens to the music of his neighbour
Suffocatingly loud
Whose stereo is the loudest?
I laugh.
Girls dance,
Youths watch.
The old people drink coffee, sitting on the floor by the doorway
Whiling the day away, Romani style.
In front of Shecho's house sit ten Roma
They form a large circle seated on the ground.
What are they doing?
I approach and see a large pan between them
Filled with roasted meat and freshly-baked bread.
They tear the bread by hand,
And eat red tomatoes,
while quaffing down strong whisky,
Together.

Like true Roma.
They see me and call out,
"Sit down sister! Eat with us!"
I sit and eat
Along with them.
I am happy.

Suno I.

Ande mrni Romani Mahala sem.
O drom Dajanli Osmanbega pe Gorica.
Bahtali sem.
Pasha mande bihuladine chava.
Mahalake, bihuladine, bahtale, Romane chava.
Savore pasha mande.
Bahtali sem.
Hi-man but kotorvale bombone.
Melale cikne vasta roden len.
Tate, kale jakha mangen len.
Shukar, lole muja halen len.
Savore Roma san kote ande Mahala.
Khonik na cherel buchi.
Sar sajekh.
Sa opash si shukar.
Phiraven kotorvale Romnjake dimije thaj
Phure kotorvale Romane gada.
Prasten pharade, prnange Romane chava.
Tate Romane ila.
Opash shulavdimata.
Opash chororipe.
Melalo, praxalo, chororo, kotorvalo thaj bahtalo.
But Roma beshen tele pe phuvjate
Phenden thaj xasajven.
Andaro sako cher ashunav aver Romani muzika.
Krlalo si.
Kahche kasetofono si majzuralo?
Xasajvav.
Cheja chelen.
Chava diklen.
Phure pijen kafava thaj beshen avri tele pasha udareste.
Romano chejfo.
Pasha Shechosko cher beshen desh Roma.
Beshen tele ande bari rota.
So cheren?
Avav pashe the dikhav bari tepsija mashkare len.
Ande tepsija peklo mas the peklo Romano marno.
Romano marno e vastenca chinden,
Lolo paradajzo halen.
Jagali rachija pijen.
Jekhethane.

Chacho Romano.
Von dikhen man, von akharen man.
Besh kate, phenorije! Xa manca!
Me beshav thaj xav.
Jekhethane lenca.
Bahtali sem.

dukh

pain

Dream II.

I go home.
The door is open.
No one is home.
Mother! Father!
No one responds.
Sisters! Brother!
No one answers.
The house door is open.
Perhaps they've gone to my uncle.
I go and check.
They're not there.
My family is gone.
There's no one.
I re-enter my house
I sit down.
I prepare coffee and drink it alone.
I see everything as it was:
Soup on the stove,
Roasted meat in a pan,
Salad and baked bread on the low Turkish table
I eat the soup prepared by my mother
And go out the door
The sun is scorching.
Maybe they went to the Turbe[4].
I pass through the upper part of the Quarter
Leading to the Turbe.
There are no Roma in the Quarter
I pass by the homes
Of Alija, Lafita, and Husica,
Nura and Selma.
I look inside, wanting to see Meha and Safija Sejdic
Their cab sits in front of the entry.
Smoke rises from the stovepipe
They're cooking for the grandchildren again
But there are no Roma.
I get up and proceed.
On my left are garages
and on their roofs, old auto parts
and scrap iron.

---

[4] *Turbe*: a meadow in which old tombs were left from the Turkish Empire.

Water gushes from the taps
Someone's pipes are broken again.
I walk slowly because I really want
to observe the Quarter.
Once more my gaze follows the houses,
now to the right
I pass the house where Bajro and Grozda Tahirovic lived.
Now Refik and his family live there — Kosovar Roma.
New Roma have come to the Quarter.
I go on and come to the tiny house
of old Muste and Zejfa
A brother and sister who never married
They know how to fight and swear like no one else on earth.
They are the best.
But there are no Roma.
Between these two houses lies the way to the small home
Of Bajro Pujpica and Ljubica Besic, Ema and
Ramo Mrvica and Celo Tahirovic.
I continue on.
Here lives Bajro Tahirovic, and beside him
Mejra and Tale, Hajra and Bugar Sejdic,
Raba and Ramiz Besic,
and the home of the family Hasanovic.
But there are no Roma.
The Quarter is empty.
I go on, crying.
I see the Turbe.
Father's car isn't here.
I leave behind the house that belongs to
Iso and Hajra, and the son Kemo.
They aren't there either.
I look down and among the shacks
where Kaja and Paso lived, Cina and Musa,
Tuna and Trajan with their children.
So much garbage around the shacks!
Ripped, old, dirty skirts and dresses,
Filthy, tattered shoes, spoiled food and paper.
Continuing on, I see a tent.
A ripped, pathetic, poor man's tent.
Kaja sits before it, as usual.

A fire burns
In front of it, a piece of sheet metal
And on the metal sits a Turkish pot
black coffee inside.
Good little Kaja.

She kisses me.
In the shade of the tent sleep five children
I sit and drink coffee with Kaja.
I want to ask about my family
And where they have gone.
Fear takes away my voice.
Menacing sounds of aircraft above!
I tremble with fright
My blood freezes.
Kaja and the children scatter.
Grenades! Bombs!
I awake startled
in a foreign land.

dukh

Suno II.

Dzav chere.
Putardo udar.
Dikhav andre.
Chucho cher.
Daje! Dade!
Khonik na irisarel.
Phenjalen! Phrala!
Khonik na irisarel.
Putardo amaro udar?!
Shaj ka avel von beshen e kakonsa.
Dzav te dikhav.
Naj san kote. Nane mi familija.
Dzav pale ando mrno cher.
Andre sem. Beshav.
Cherav kafava pala pes.
Dikhav kaj sa si sar sasa:
Zumi ande chiradija,
Peklo mas ande bari tepsija
Salata thaj marno pe sinija.
Hav dejaki zumi.
Avri sem.
O kham zuralo tatarel.
Ali naj len Roma ande Mahala.
Phiravav krzo Mahala koring Turbe.
Shaj te avel von beshen kote.
Mukhav e chera kaj dzuvden: Alija, Latifa thaj Husica,
phuri Nura thaj Selma.
Dikhav prdal pe kaj mangav te dikhav phure Meho thaj Safija.
Lesko fijakero si avri pasho cher.
Andaro sulundaro del o thuv.
Von chiraven hape pala chavoreske chavoren.
Sar sajekh.
Ali naj len Roma ande Mahala.
Phiravav.
Pe mrno stingo rig san but garazhurje,
Opre phure vordoneske kotora thaj phuro sastro.

Chesmava anadari savi o paj biachado del thav.
Phiravav polohko mangav lungo te dikhav sako shej,
sako cher ande Mahala.
Me jakha dzan pale pe chacho rig.
Mukhav o cher kaj beshile Bajro thaj Grozda.
Akana kote beshel o Refiko e familijenca, Kosovako Rom.
E Roma paruven ande Mahala.
Phiravav thaj dikhav cikni cher kaj trajen phure Zejfa thaj Muste,
phen thaj phral save nikana na maritimen.
Von dzanen te chingaren thaj akushen sar khonik.
Po majlacho.
Ali naj len Roma ande Mahala.
Mashkare si o dromorro savo anel tut dziko cikno cher.
Kote beshen Bajro Pujpica thaj Ljubica,
Ema thaj Ramo Mrvica, Chelo Tahirovic.
Phiravav durder.
Kote si o cher kaj beshel Baja Tahirovic, pasha si Mejra thaj Tale,
Hajra thaj Bugar Sejdic, Raba thaj Ramiz Beshic,
o cher kaj beshel familija Hasanovic.
Ali naj len Roma ande Mahala.
Chuchi Mahala.
Phiravav.
Rovav.
Akana dikhav Turbe.
Nane dadesko vordon.
Nakhalav o cher kaj trajen Iso thaj Hajra.
Phiravav durder thaj tele talo dromeste si baraka kaj trajen
Kaja thaj Pasho, Musa thaj Cina, Tuna thaj Trajan e familijenca.
Opash baraka si shulavdimata:
phure, melale thaj pharade cohe thaj gada,
melale thaj pharade kundure, hape thaj papirja.
A naj len Roma ande Mahala.
Dzav dromenca thaj dikhav cahra.
Pharadi cahra.
Chorori cahra.
Pandz chavoren soven kote.
Romni Kaja beshel kote.

Laki jag si dzuvdi.
Pe jagate dzezva,
Ande dzezva kali kafava.

Kaja chumidel man.
Beshav te pijav kafava.
Mangav te phuchav pala mrni familija.
Daravipe chinel mrni vorba.
Sastrune chirikle!!!.
Izdrav e daravipestar.
Chavoren thaj Kaja nashaven.
Granaturja, bombe!!!
Sar o bar sem.
Nashti te nashavav e daravipestar.
Kaj si mrni familija?
Granaturja, bombe!!!
Vazdav ando parno themeste……

pain

Wind

MORNING
The wind of God carries away my troubles.
The wind of God blows in my hopes.

AFTERNOON
The water of St. George cleanses my illness.
The fragrance of hyacinths creates beauty for me.

NIGHT
Bright slender candles burn
Shining in Romani windows.
The aroma of halva and prayers waft through the air
I am healed in my Quarter, this night of Mubarek.

The wind of God soothes me.
The wind of God lulls me to sleep.

Balval

TEHARIN
Devlesko Balval phurdel mo phraripe
Devlesko Balval idjarel mo dozacharipe.

OPASHODJIVE
Djurdjevdansko pajorro thovel mo nasvalipe.
Zumbulako sung del mandje shukaripe.

JRAT
Kotorvale, cikne memela phabaren.
Romane pendzera strafinen.
Halvako sung the Devlesko rudjipe krzo hava buhljaren.
Mahala the mubarek jrat man sastiven.

Devlesko Balval kushljarel man
Devlesko Balval sovljarel man.

Why?

If the sky has eyes,
If the wind has hands,
If the sun warms man,
Why is the Rom freezing?

If non-Roma make wars,
If they pass laws,
If non-Rom respect all people,
Why are Roma dying like dogs?

If the sky has eyes,
If the wind has hands,
If God loves mankind,
Why are the Roma crying?

The sky is opening.
The sun is fleeing.
The wind is moaning.
And a flower is crying,
Along with the Roma.

Sose?

Ako o del hi-leh e jakha,
Ako o balval hi-leh e vasta,
Ako o kham e manushen tatarel,
Sose o Rom shilajvel?

Ako o gadzo cherel e maripa,
Ako vov cherel e krisipa,
Ako o gadzo sa manushen pale pachavel,
Sose o Rom sar o dzukela merel?

Ako o del hi-leh e jakha,
Ako o balval hi-leh e vasta,
Ako o Devel e manushen kamel,
Sose o Rom rovel?

O del putaravel.
O kham nashavel.
O balval riknjavel.
I luludji e Romenca rovel.

The Earth

Romnije[5]!
Romnije!
Because of all the dead and all the living,
Because of the Roma,
Put a curse on the Earth
To destroy the rats
To destroy the enemy.

Romnije!
Because of all the dead and all the living,
Because of the Roma
Turn the Earth upside down
And predict black destiny
To distract the devil[6]
To distract the black night.

Romnije!
Because of all the dead and all the living,
Because of the Roma
Cast magic upon the Earth and predict love.
Predict a fire without smoke
Predict damnation with the end.

Cast a magic spell, Romnije, save her!
She is yours, she is mine, Mother of God
THE EARTH.

---

[5] *romnije*: roma women.
[6] i.e.: evil forces

Phuv

Romnije!
Pala mule thaj dzuvinde,
Pala e Roma,
Del armaja e phuvjache,
Te nashjares shimijake
Te nashjares dushmaja.

Romnije!
Pala mule thaj dzuvinde,
Pala e Roma,
Chuv teleshoreha e phuv
Thaj del armaja kale sudbinache
Te xoxajves bilache
Te xoxajves kali jrat.

Romnije!
Pala mule thaj dzuvinde,
Pala e Roma,
Del e phuvjache choxanipe thaj del cho mrtik pala o kamipe
Nek e jag na thuvljardel
Nek o dumutnipe na buhljarel.

Del o chohanipe, Romnije, del cho mrtik pala las
Voj si chiri, mrni thaj Devleski dej
PHUV.

I Will Die For You

Whether the sun is shining or the rain is falling
Whether birds are twittering or the wind is blowing
Whether I am laughing or crying
I sense you — I want you.

And you,
You walk right past me,
You don't see me,
You don't care about me.
May God strike me dead! I will bind you to me.
With seven chains, I will bind you.
Seven drops of my blood I will spill
Upon the earth you trod.
May God strike me! I shall bewitch you.
I will cast a love spell
And if you don't come to me anyway
I will draw your strength into the smoke of my fire.
Come here, come with me, sleep with me
My wicked love.
May God strike me dead! I will die for you.

Ka Merav Pala Tute

O kham kana tatarel, jal brshind kana perel
E chirikli kana chichirel, jal o balval kana phurdel
Kana hasajvav, jal kana rovav
Me hacharav tut. Me mangav tut.

A tu,
Tu phiraves pasha mande,
Na dikhes man,
Na manges man.
Te marel ma o Del! Me ka phandav tut.
E efta lancurjenca ka phendav tut.
E efta kavchina e mrne ratestar ka chudav
Pe phuvjache kaj phiraves tut.
Te marel ma o Del! Te ka bendjarav tut.
Ako ka cherav o bendjalipe
Ako na aves mansa
Ka thovav tuche zor ande mi jagehchi thuv.
Av kate, av mansa, sov pasha mande
Mo bendjalo kamipe.
Te marel ma o Del! Ka merav pala tute.

I Have To Go From Here

My voice is imprisoned
I can't talk
My soul is in pain.
Bitter tears.
Bitter memory.
My Romani Quarter.
Gorica, Sarajevo.
I am imprisoned within myself.
I am sick with loneliness.
For the Roma, my people.

My voice is imprisoned
I cannot speak
My soul is in pain
Bitter tears.
Bitter memory.
My Romani family.
Bosnia.
A hundred questions, no one answer.
A hundred dreams, no one reality.
I have to go from here.
I have to be there.
I have to get better.

Mora Te Dzav-Tar Katar

Mrno krlo si phanglo,
Nashti te vacharav
E pharipestar.
Cherchale jasva.
Cherchale hacharipa.
Mrni Romani Mahala.
Gorica, Sarajevo.
Phangli sem ando peste.
Nasvali sem e korkoripestar.
Roma, mrno narodo.

Mrno krlo si phanglo
Nashti te vacharav
E pharipestar.
Cherchale jasva.
Cherchale hacharipa.
Mrni Romani familija.
Bosna.
Shel phuchipengo nane jekh irisaripe.
Shel sunengo nane chachipe.
Mora te dzav-tar katar.
Mora te dzav kote.
Mora te sastivav.

dukh

pain

A Deceased Good Rom

In the room lies
A deceased, good Rom,
Around him, Roma are sitting
To speak to him one last time.
Women and children have gone
To Uncle's house.
A deceased, good Rom
Should sleep in peace.
The window is slightly open
And the door is closed.
By the window, a glass.
In the glass, cold water.
At the window, a plate.
In the plate, white flour.
A deceased, good Rom
Should eat one last time.
A deceased, good Rom
Should not go hungry
Into the second world.
Television and mirror are covered.
A young man
Prays and cries
With the Roma all night.
The sun is rising
Morning is awakening.
At the window a bird is chirping.
In the glass is less water
In the plate the trail of fingers.
The deceased, good Rom ate
One last time.
A funeral car comes
And the deceased, good Rom is driven away
All the Roma from the Quarter are outside,
They pour water out from pails
And pray together
For the deceased, good Rom:
"Go with water!
Go with God!"

Mulo Lacho Rom

Ande soba pashljel
mulo lacho Rom,
Opash les Roma beshen
thaj lesa phenden agoresko drom.
Romnja thaj chava dzele
ando kakosko cher,
Mulo lacho Rom
Trubuj ando miro te sovel.
Pendzero si putardo thaj
udar phanglo.
Pe pendzero taxtaj.
Ande taxtaj paj shudro.
Pe pendzero tijari.
Ande tijari aro parno.
Mulo lacho Rom
trubuj te hal agoresko drom.
Mulo lacho Rom
na trubuj te dzal
pe dujto them bokhalo.
Ucharde san televizija thaj dikhlo
E Romenca sasto jrat
bandjavel thaj rovel
terno raklo.
O kham iklovel,
Teharin avel,
Pe pendzero chirikli chicharel.
Ande taxtaj pohari paj
Ande tijari vurma kataro naj.
Halo mulo lacho Rom
agoresko drom.
E mulesko vordon avel
Thaj mulo lacho Rom anel.
Sa Roma ande Mahala avri ikloven,
O paj andare kachunende chordardiven,
The krlalo jekhethane
pala mulo lacho Rom rudjisaven:
"Dza pajeha!
Dza Devleha!"

dukh   *pain*

Thanks · Pari Kerav Pala

Naomi Binder Wall
Lynn Hutchinson
Florence Gibson
Paul St. Clair
Ronald Lee

Coming in 2008 from
MAGORIA BOOKS

THE LIVING FIRE
(E Zhivindi Yag)

BY RONALD LEE

Ronald Lee's autobiographical novel, formerly published as "Goddam Gypsy", is an intense, fast moving, and brutally honest affair.

Yanko—a Canadian Rom who 'took the non-Gypsy way but didn't go far'—seeks his fortunes both among and apart from the Roma, never quite finding his place. His story exposes the out of sight, out of mind world of Canada's Roma in 1970's Montréal: Parties, rackets, bar brawls, weddings, desperate poverty, and intermittent police raids fuel in Yanko the passion, creativity, and rebellious defiance that is The Living Fire.

MAGORIA BOOKS
www.MagoriaBooks.com

Coming in 2008 from
MAGORIA BOOKS

LEGENDS OF THE ROMA
(working title)

BY HEDINA TAHIROVIĆ SIJERČIĆ

A unique collection of Romani legends and folktales bring alive the rich cultural and religious traditions of the Roma.

Formerly published in English and German under the title "Romany Legends", Magoria Books plans to make the book available both as an English and Romani language edition aimed at adult audiences, as well as a series of richly illustrated full-colour children's books.

Visit our website for updates on this and other projects.

MAGORIA BOOKS
www.MagoriaBooks.com

About Magoria Books

Magoria Books is an independent Canadian publisher specializing in Romani books. Our aim is to provide Romani authors with opportunities to present and thereby preserve the culture, language, and folklore of the Roma.

Magoria Books would therefore like to encourage Romani poets, writers, and activists to approach us with their ideas and proposals. We are particularly interested in folktales, poetry, and manuscripts written in the Romani language; but are open to considering other materials.

We are also interested in partnerships with translators, community organizations, and foreign publishers to find ways to increase distribution, availability, and relevance of existing and upcoming titles.

Write to us at:

Magoria Books
1562 Danforth Avenue #92006
Toronto, ON M4J 5C1
Canada

www.ingramcontent.com/pod-product-compliance
Ingram Content Group UK Ltd.
Pitfield, Milton Keynes, MK11 3LW, UK
UKHW041424180426
11947UKWH00007B/277